Cons

Northern Virginia's Home Selling Survival Guide

Third Edition

Steve Bradley

TABLE OF CONTENTS

INTRODUCTION 5
1 WHY PEOPLE THINK REALTORS® SUCK 7
2 THREE MISTAKES SELLERS MUST AVOID....................................... 13
3 SEVEN CRITICAL WAYS SELLERS LOSE MONEY 19
4 CHOOSING THE RIGHT REALTOR® TO SELL YOUR HOME 23
5 ELEVEN PROBING INTERVIEW QUESTIONS FOR REALTORS® 39
6 GETTING YOUR HOME READY FOR THE MARKET 45
7 PRICING YOUR HOME TO SELL NOT SIT 57
8 MARKETING YOUR HOME FOR SALE 67
9 SHOWING YOUR HOME 73
10 WORKING WITH OFFERS 77
11 CLOSING YOUR SALE... 85
12 SELLING AND BUYING AT THE SAME TIME……………………….. 93
BONUS CHAPTER: REALTOR® LIES AND MISDIRECTION 103
CONCLUSION… 117
LIMITS OF LIABILITY & DISCLAIMER OF WARRANTY 119
COPYRIGHT 121
HOW TO CONTACT THE AUTHOR.. 123

3

Introduction

Selling a home can be daunting, but I am still surprised at how often I meet sellers who have tried to sell their house before and failed. Many homeowners simply don't realize the complexity of finding the right REALTOR®, preparing their home, showing their home, negotiating the contract, and dealing with all the moving parts that can break along the way.

As a REALTOR® who has been a *listing agent* his entire career, my goal for this book is to share my experience and offer advice to homeowners that want to sell their home. *Listing agents* specialize in working with sellers, and they bring a higher level of understanding to what it takes to get a home sold.

The listing agent that you choose to help sell your home is the critical linchpin to all the steps and processes along the way, including preparing your home, setting your price, negotiating your contract terms, and then managing what can often be a winding road to closing.

Don't become another failed home sale in your area. Homeowners need to understand the dynamics of selling, the steps to qualifying the right agent, and the preparation needed before walking the long road to the closing process.

If you have any real estate related questions, or wish to set up a free, no-obligation consultation, I am available. Please do not hesitate to contact me. In the meantime, I hope you read this book before you make any big decisions.

Here's to Your Success!

Steve Bradley

1
Why People Think REALTORS® Suck

This topic could take up a whole book all by itself. There are blogs, websites and memes dealing specifically with this topic.

It's relatively easy to get your real estate license, but it is *not* easy to become a highly successful real estate agent. It takes time and a lot of experience. Also, most real estate agents work part-time. Read that again: Most real estate agents work part-time! No wonder they have trouble. And they do!

Can you imagine hiring a part-time doctor who also works as a landscaper to supplement her income? Do you think she could be a great doctor and a highly experienced one if she needs a second job? What about her availability to answer calls from her patients or other doctors, nurses or caretakers? As a principal broker, I have seen deals collapse over something that could have been avoided if the agent had just answered and returned calls in a timely manner.

Real estate agents sometimes have a reputation as being sleazy or greedy or unreliable – and only interested in how much money they can make. Yes, they are out there, and I can tell who they are just by looking at how they represent homeowners' homes that they have listed in the MLS (Multiple Listing Service). In my opinion, if an agent is not willing to invest their money in your property to help get it sold, they are stealing from you at the very start.

In any profession, you have the good, the bad and the ugly. The Pareto Principal (named after Italian economist and sociologist Vilfredo Pareto) is famous for the 80/20 rule. I find that, in real estate, it becomes the 90/10 rule. Basically, 10% of the agents are producing 90% of the local sales, and the other 90% aren't doing anything except keeping you from finding a great agent! The odds are stacked against you when it comes to finding the best REALTOR®.

In fact, the lower 90% of agents are averaging less than four closed sales a year. So, someone who falls into that 90% category and has been licensed for five years has probably closed about 20 sales in all that time. That isn't nearly enough closings for the agent to have learned even the basic ins and outs of selling a home or how to deal with the major problems that often need to be solved during the sale process. And the issues increase exponentially if the agent on the other side (the one who is helping the buyer) is *also* an inexperienced agent.

Adding to this confusion is the fact that, in July of every

year, there are changes to the Virginia real estate laws, and the related documents change as well. Part-time and inexperienced agents often have no clue about the changes, and nor do they have the time to attend the classes that are held to educate them on the changes. Basically, they are 'faking it until they make it' and hoping you don't notice this while they learn their trade trying to represent you. These inexperienced and often unsupervised agents are a good reason the public has such a low opinion of REALTORS®. Meanwhile, the homeowners who are selling feel short-changed; they realize they have paid way too much for the minimal guidance they received. And they are 100% correct in that assessment.

Unfortunately, it's difficult to find out *who* the top 10 percent of real estate agents are, and even then, they are often so busy that they treat you like a number rather than a person or family managing a very large financial – and also emotional – transaction. Later in this book, I will share what I feel is the 'sweet spot' for the number of transactions per year that gets you a great agent – one who is highly experienced and who will be 100% involved in selling your home.

Home sellers tend to hire based on some of the shakiest qualifications imaginable. Then they wonder why their agent is not effective and why their home doesn't sell – or maybe worse: why it sold and they lost so much money in the process.

Part-time agents are typically less stable financially. Even with the best of intentions, they can be motivated by a paycheck and lose sight of protecting your best interest.

Furthermore, new and inexperienced agents – because there are so many of them – can make the profession look bad. By default, those agents who *are* professional and highly experienced can be lumped into the group of agents who are unprofessional and lacking in knowledge and experience.

Besides full-time agents and part-time agents, there are real estate 'mega teams' that are just revolving doors for home sales. I call them the *Walmart* of real estate; their volume is so high that customer service is basically an afterthought. I remember meeting a buyer agent for one of our local mega teams and she shared that the owner of the team generated so much volume that there was *zero effort* put into following up with clients to see how the process was going. In and out – that's all the team cared about.

Any good team will have a group of people working for you and your sale. But these mega clearing-house agents often don't even speak to their client – you the homeowner. You are always dealing with someone else and left feeling that you aren't important. When it's all done, you realize that you have never even spoken to the one agent who made most of the money.

A huge compliment I hear from sellers regarding their completed home sale using myself and my team is that they were treated like they were my *only* client. I love that it comes through like that to my clients. As a homeowner, you should never feel like a *number* with your home selling team. It's critical for your agent to have a support team, but your agent must be there for you and fully understand how to best sell your home.

Have faith! In this book, I am going to share critical information to help you select the *best* real estate agent, one who will help you sell your home in a reasonable time frame and for top dollar.

2
Three Mistakes Sellers Must Avoid

As the thought of selling your home starts to churn in your head, there are three important mistakes you must avoid if you want to make it to the other side with the most money in your pocket.

Mistake #1 - Not knowing why you are selling

When I meet with sellers and they start off with: "we don't have to sell but if we get a good offer we are okay selling," I immediately find a polite way to address the fact that their *motivation* for selling is key. If they have no idea why, or are just testing the waters, then it's probably not the best time to sell.

As a professional real estate listing agent, I've seen homeowners put homes on the market without any thought about why; and they almost always price very high for the market 'just to try it out.' Inevitably, they don't sell or they must drop their price often and lose money when it comes to the final offer. What the seller is unaware of is that the details of their failed sale, and even their continuing price drops, are all permanent records in the MLS. If the house doesn't sell and then comes on the market again a year or two later, any REALTOR® representing a potential buyer will have quick access to these details. Why is that a big deal? Because buyers will believe that the seller must be desperate, given that they were unable to sell the first time. So typically, the buyer will offer much less for the home even if it is now priced properly.

So, think carefully and have a good *reason* to sell, or just wait until the time is right for you to finally move forward with selling.

Do not be surprised if a REALTOR® you interview turns down working with you to sell your home if you 'don't have to sell.' Real estate agents do not get paid until they fulfill their commitment to you and get you to the closing table. This involves a significant amount of time, money, knowledge and resources. Why would they invest all of that if you don't need to sell and have no particular motivation? Would you go to work for two or three months if you knew the project was likely to be cancelled and your boss wouldn't pay you for that time? You would not find that acceptable, so don't expect a REALTOR® to be okay with that likely outcome if you 'don't have to sell.'

Mistake #2 - Hiring a REALTOR® Based on the List Price They Suggest to You

I talked earlier about REALTORS® who are 'sleazy' or not professional at what they do. Well, this is one of their tricks of the trade: they try to win the listing from a seller by promising them a high listing price. Why would they do this if it won't sell at that price? First, it's because they just want to get the listing agreement signed. Then very quickly after the signing, they will try to convince the seller that the market has changed and that they need to adjust their price if they want to sell.

The other strategy that really brings a lot of value to the agent is just having a sign in your yard. Yes, this is actually a 'thing.' That For Sale sign in the yard and the online listing are powerful tools for a REALTOR®. Together they generate a lot of buyer lead calls to the listing agent. The goal for the REALTOR® is to generate as many buyer leads as he can before you eventually want to fire him. This makes that signed listing worth it to him even when it never sells.

A third value to that sleazy agent is that the sign in the yard is seen by all your neighbors and by people driving by. As the agent starts to market to the area for new listings, the sign adds further validation for potential clients. Eventually, the agent could generate, on average, 2-4 leads and 1-2 closings from these efforts.

Never allow an agent's *suggested* list price to influence your selection of agents. Make them present the data to support their suggested listing price. If you really don't know the value of your home, pay for an appraisal and take some of the mystery out of it.

Mistake #3: Hiring a REALTOR® Based on Their Compensation Amount

We all understand the desire to save money, and in a home sale, the money can really add up. The money saved is relative to what you get for it. If you are looking for a cheap knock-off Rolex® watch, you'll go hit the street vendors in DC. But if you want a great example of a timeless Rolex® or Tag Heuer®, you know that you need to find a reputable store and that you are going to pay a premium to get the best.

Selecting an agent can be a bit similar to that. To explain, let me use my tax accountant example that I am famous for. Of course, everyone wants a great deal: we buy when items are on sale; we 'buy one get one free'; we are attracted to 'bargains.' But in real estate, you're not purchasing a watch, a suit or an expensive handbag. You need someone who is a true master at what they do – a professional. So, here's my example: Every year we all file our federal and state taxes. Which accountant would you select from the following scenarios?

Scenario one: You find two accountants. Accountant 1 charges $400 and Accountant 2 charges $800. Who would you pick? Not knowing anything else about them, you would select Accountant 1 for $400.

Scenario two: Accountant 1 works part time while Accountant 2 works full time. Who would you pick? Most people would still pick Accountant 1 because not knowing anything else, the $400 savings compared to Accountant 2 is too hard to ignore.

Scenario three: Accountant 1 has only been working two years and is not a CPA. Accountant 2 has been in business 10 years and is a CPA. Who would you pick? Now it's getting harder. Now people are being reminded of the value of an experienced professional. Smart people that understand the complexities they need help with will pick Accountant 2, but still a high number will select Accountant 1 because of the $400 difference.

Scenario four: What if you could look into the future and then come back to the present and make the best choice? In this scenario, Tax Accountant 1 works part time, has been working for two years, is not a certified public accountant, and has no past online customer reviews. She charges you $400 to do your family taxes, but later you find that she completely missed over $10,000 in deductions, and due to her sloppy practices, you end up getting audited later. Tax Accountant 2 is full time, has been in business 10 years, is a CPA, and has rave reviews from past clients.

Tax Accountant 2 charges $800 to do your family taxes. Due to her experience, she finds that $10,000 in deductions that Accountant 1 would have missed; she offers suggestions on how to save even more money the following year; and you don't end up getting audited. Now I ask you: who would you pick? You would be crazy not to pick Accountant 2, knowing that her education, the fact that she works full time, and her years of experience play into the final results and into the reviews from past clients.

Her past clients will tell you that paying the $800 for the right accountant saved them literally thousands of dollars. Not to mention the potential legal issues that can come up if one uses an inexperienced accountant in the hope of getting the cheapest deal upfront.

Selecting the *right* real estate professional is of critical importance. Spend time qualifying them. Read their reviews. Ask them the interview questions I have shared here in Chapter 5. And don't be tricked by discount agents that thrive on volume and the fast close with no regard for what is best for you or your bottom-line.

3
Seven Critical Ways Sellers Lose Money

Losing money can happen at many different junctures when you are selling a home. For most home sellers, the greatest potential for the highest loss of money is #7 on my list. So, let's count them down, or in this case, up.

The *first* critical time you lose money in a real estate transaction is when you're <u>preparing your home</u> or when you don't prepare it at all. Make certain to take the time to prepare and stage your house properly, and to listen to your REALTOR's staging advice. This is a critical point and I see a lot of people doing their preparation at different stages of their selling process. I suggest you get it all done *before* listing your home.

Very often, I'll have a seller who says: "I want to be on the market by this weekend, so let me get these major items done and I'll finish the rest over the next couple of weeks while the home is active on the market." My response to that is:

"You're throwing money away. Get it all done *before* you list." You're much better off waiting a week than not having your staging completed prior to being listed. So, pay attention to the suggestions from your REALTOR® (who you've chosen carefully); you'll be glad that you did.

The *second* critical time you lose money in a real estate transaction is when you're pricing your home for the market. If you price too high, nobody views your home, you chase the market down, and you end up losing a lot more money than if you would have priced properly in the beginning. Chasing the market happens when the seller's current price is always higher than the market will pay. This occurs when a seller prices high initially, and then after a long time not selling, they reduce their price. The problem is that sellers never make the full reduction that is needed. When the market needed them to drop by $20,000, they only dropped by $10,000. The cycle repeats, no offer is received, they need to reduce, and again they make a partial adjustment. By the time the seller has accepted the fact that they should be $20,000 lower than their starting price, it's too late. The market sees their home as damaged goods because of how long it's been on the market. Any offer that comes in at this point will almost always be lower than their final adjusted price. If the seller would have priced properly at the start, they would not have lost all that money chasing the market. Talk to your real estate agent about what it is to 'chase the market' and they will share with you, in painful detail, how many times they've seen a seller lose money in this process. On the other hand, if you price too low, you end up having people that offer you even less money because they think you're desperate to sell fast.

The *third* critical time that you lose money in a real estate transaction is during the offer negotiation phase. You want to make sure you have a seasoned real estate listing team on your side that has negotiated more than just a few contracts. For example, sometimes a buyer needs seller help on closing costs, and if your agent doesn't know how to offer a solution that helps the buyer, but at the same time doesn't lose you money, then you either lose the buyer or lose the money. You need a seasoned professional to help you through the difficult terms that are included in an offer and make sure you don't lose money in the process.

The *fourth* critical time that you lose money in a real estate transaction is during the inspections. This may seem obvious, but this is where I see thousands of dollars disappear for some homeowners. Make certain to take the time to consider your options. These are items that can be negotiated, so take your time to figure out what your response is going to be. Listen to the advice of your real estate agent, but they should also be listening to *you* so as to get the best results and save you from losing money during this phase.

The *fifth* critical time you can lose money during a real estate transaction is during the buyer's appraisal. If the buyer's appraisal comes in below the contract price, they probably have the option to void the offer based on that. If they do void, you will have lost money based on having to put your house back on the market, and you're going to have to pay additional mortgage payments and utilities as well as HOA fees or association fees. Another point to make here is that you definitely want to ensure that you have planned ahead of time and that you have the ability to respond to a low appraisal. A good listing team will provide you with options regarding how to respond to a low appraisal as well as other issues.

The *sixth* critical time you can lose money in a real estate transaction is right at the end of the process, during the buyer's walkthrough. While this process is different from state to state, it's still an opportunity, if there's a major problem found, for the buyer to come to you and try to negotiate on issues that need to be dealt with, such as repairs that weren't immediately obvious. If your REALTOR® doesn't have the experience to manage this type of scenario, you could find yourself losing more money at the closing table.

The *seventh* – and to me the most critical – time that you can lose money is before you ever list your home for sale. It is when you select your REALTOR®. In Chapter 5, I share the best questions to ask agents when you interview them, and I share some details that most sellers are not aware of. The more you know, the more successful you will be in selecting a REALTOR® that is *the best fit for you*. Selecting the wrong listing agent can spell doom to your home sale and profits. Your listing agent is the key to managing items 1 through 6 on this list. If they lack the experience, confidence and knowhow, you will become another statistic, another homeowner that lost big while trying to sell.

4
Choosing the Right REALTOR® to Sell Your Home

Let us take a step back for a moment and think about why you hire a real estate agent to help you sell your home.

To select the best listing agent for your home, you need to first think of *why* you are hiring this person and *what* you expect of them. In this chapter, I will share with you what my years of being a listing agent have taught me regarding what sellers need to look for and what they truly need to get the highest dollar amount for their home.

Most sellers need four critical services from their real estate agent. Keep these in mind as you search for a listing agent to help you sell your home.

1. Home Preparation & Staging Support
2. Research & Price Setting

3. Marketing Expertise
4. Negotiating & Contract Skills

Area #1: Home Preparation & Staging Support

A great agent can step up and start saving you money well before you ever list your home for sale. Experienced listing agents can walk your property outside and inside and find a ton of great free or inexpensive ideas that keep you from losing money later due to home inspection challenges; and that, at the same time, increase your home's value to buyers. Often, even a few hundred dollars here or there can add thousands of dollars back into your pocket. You want an agent with the experience to provide this type of insight.

Often when I meet with sellers, they have grandiose upgrading or renovation plans that they are thinking about implementing prior to selling. When I caution them that they probably won't get their money back in the sale, they seem confused – as if it's a certainty that their home's value will increase exponentially. However, it's often not a great idea to do serious renovations. Talk with your agent first and find out how the market is reacting to homes already for sale and how they compare to your home.

Sometimes a seller, not knowing any better and not consulting with his listing agent, completes major upgrades thinking that he will earn twice what he paid for them when he sells the house – and thinking that it will make his home worth more than a similar home that has just sold down the street. But this may not be the case.

Qualify that your agent has the experience to help you identify the key areas needing attention before you start doing any work at all.

In my listing practice, I always take pictures when I visit the home, and then I return with a detailed list of repairs and staging advice to accompany the photos. This gives my seller a checklist to go by and they can get their home ready with a detailed plan of attack.

If you are not sure if the agent you are speaking with has the skill to advise you regarding repairs and staging, ask them for links to past homes they have sold. Our MLS has data going back a long time. If your agent tells you the photos are gone now that the listing is sold, they are lying to you. For example, it is a very simple process for us to login to our MLS backend and send the seller an email with links to past listings.

Look at the photos. Does the home look attractive and well prepared? Does it look staged and ready for showings? Or are these photos showing junk, clothes, boxes and messy rooms? Are the photos professional, or do they look like they were taken with a cell phone?

In the end, the seller decides what they will and will not do, but you should still see an overall theme of clean, staged photos that show the home in its best light. Staging is key to great photos and a great online presence.

Area #2: Research & Price Setting

Sellers are looking to their listing agent for direction on what they should list their home for. If you have a price in mind regarding how much you think you want for the home, never be afraid to share that with your REALTOR®. They are working *for* you, not against you.

Messing up on your listing price can spell havoc for your home selling plans. Yes, there is a lot of data online, but that data is typically just *wrong*. These large website portals that promise free estimates of value are not even close to what a buyer will pay for your home. You cannot set a target listing price without going into the home in question and then comparing it to the recent closed sales in the area that are comparable to this home.

My preference is to get inside as many of the homes we will be competing against as we can. This gives us real data and lets us craft a perfect listing price.

The ability to properly price a home from the start is critical. Pricing high means you will not sell or you will experience a huge loss of money when you do. As the seller starts to drop the price, they almost never make the full drop needed on the first price adjustment. They still believe in their price and of course that is their prerogative. But the reality is that by the time they get to the proper price, the damage has been done. Any buyer that would have snatched the home up if it were priced correctly at the start has moved on. If they are still looking, they may now have decided that this particular homeowner is unreasonable and will be difficult to deal with, so they pass the home over completely.

I hear buyers make this exact comment so often. Typically, buyers are very savvy and know what is selling for what. They are seeing *all* the homes that you are competing with. If they don't react quickly to your home, that can be a sign of trouble long term.

Hire a REALTOR® who can show you data that supports the price they are suggesting for you. Feel free to challenge it, of course. If you cannot come to an agreement with your REALTOR®, I suggest you get in the car with your listing agent and actually go to visit your competition's homes. Go inside and see what they have. Remember that new kitchen you installed that made you think you were worth $20,000 more than everyone else? Well guess what? Often the competition has an upgraded kitchen as well. So look for the differences and try to look at these other homes and your home as if you were a buyer.

Part-time agents and those large clearing house teams typically miss the mark or purposely price low just to get an offer and get the home sold. The part-time agent needs the cash; the mega team needs the volume. Make certain that the agent you hire has the experience to help you price your home to sell. It is also important that you feel comfortable speaking openly and honestly with your agent to discuss pricing if your home is sitting without offers.

Area #3: Marketing Expertise

The MLS is not the only place where your home should be listed by your agent. Marketing a home requires a plan – a written detailed plan.

The agent that you hire must not only understand marketing, and marketing homes for sale; they must be *the best of the best*. Great marketing helps to drive traffic and attention to *your* home – over all the others competing for attention. Marketing methods change over time, so they need to be current with what works in today's home selling market.

Marketing today is very different than it was ten or even five years ago. Your agent is in a constant battle to stay informed and ahead of the competition, and to get your home sold.

Ten years ago, I used to create business card CD's that featured the home's virtual tour and a PDF home brochure. That CD was always taped to the front of the outside flyer at the signpost, and sellers and buyers absolutely loved it. It was small enough to fit in their pocket and they could watch the tour and read the information about the home at their leisure. Buyers remembered our home listings over the others in the area because of this unique feature.

Fast forward ten years, and as cool as that was, we don't do it anymore. It is just not needed and not as impactful as it was. Now all of that can be hosted online for quick access. So now we create text-to-call action. Using their smartphone, a buyer sends an advertised text message to the agent's phone. In return, the buyer receives a text with details and can quickly view virtual tours and home details right on their phone as they stand outside the home.

Your agent needs to know the current trends, which ones work best, and how to apply them. A huge problem I have with most listing agents revolves around online marketing for the home they are representing. For most of them, their 'online marketing' is placing the home in our MLS, which pushes it to other websites. And then for social media advertising, which is key now, they simply place your home onto their social media accounts and call this 'social media advertising'!

That is beyond ridiculous. Advertising on social media requires a paid approach to push your home out to *people that would buy your home*; not just anyone, and definitely not just the few hundred (if that) that follow your REALTOR®'s social media pages.

Ask your agent for a copy of their marketing plan. If they do not have one *in writing*, that is a huge red flag. Ask for samples or screenshots of social media advertising they have done, and ask them to explain the process. It is okay if it all sounds confusing to *you*, but *they* need to sound like they know what they're talking about.

You are paying good money to sell your home. The right marketing plan adds dollars to your pocket due to greater exposure, higher offer prices, and a shorter time on the market.

Area #4: Negotiating & Contract Skills

Negotiating

This is one thing that some agents forget about. They

focus on helping the seller to get the home ready, pricing the home, and marketing, and then they assume that the rest just happens. This is a huge oversight, and more so if that is what *you* are thinking as well. I will share some stories later in the book about why understanding how to negotiate and knowing the contract language can save deals from falling apart completely. In my case, this has ultimately saved my sellers thousands of dollars.

Negotiating is an art form. Some people have it and others do not. Confidence without arrogance can get the deal done and put you in the driver's seat with your home sale, and for that you need the right listing agent.

In Northern Virginia, as in all the US, there are so many new agents. Some are timid; others are over-the-top aggressive, possibly because they are trying to hide their lack of experience. A good negotiator works well with *everyone*. It is about showing the other side that you understand what they want; and it's about finding a way to craft the deal to potentially help them get some of what they want while always protecting your seller's best interests, bottom line, and terms of agreement.

For example, when a low offer comes in for your seller, a good negotiator doesn't just send back a counter offer at the original listing price. A good negotiator helps the seller counter the offer, most likely barely under the listing price, but also includes details that can help the buyer agent support the seller's counter offer.

Unfortunately, so many new and part-time seller agents

lack the knowledge and skills to do this. When you hand the buyer agent information that helps support your counter offer, they will be well informed as they discuss your response with the buyer. In the end, this is all to the seller's advantage.

Another example is when your seller is new on the market and a strong offer comes in, but the buyer wants 3% seller assistance, a credit at closing. The best tactic here is to know that the buyer *wants* the home. They have written a quick offer but financially they may need that 3% to close. Being new on the market, there is no good reason to leave money on the table. A good negotiator, knowing the buyer's high interest in the home, will offer a solution. What I would do in this case is personally call the buyer agent and explain that we like the offer but that the 3% is not in our best interest. Then I would suggest that the buyer increase their offer price by 3% and that the seller can return that as a credit at closing. This way, the buyer gets the credit they need and my seller gets the full price offer and bottom line that they deserve.

It is difficult to figure out if your listing agent is a great negotiator just by interviewing them. Possibly you could ask them if they have stories they can share on how they negotiated a win for past sellers. I also suggest that you read their online reviews. I have my clients put all my reviews up at Zillow (an online real estate database) so they are in one location and easy for people to go through.

Contract knowledge – In Northern Virginia, actually all of Virginia, the new real estate laws update in July of every year. It is paramount that your agent be focused on staying informed of the new changes and how they impact you, the seller. Also, the related documents change and that new language must be learned.

Another way to stay informed is through our REALTOR® access to the Virginia Association of REALTORS® (VAR) legal updates and their highlights of real estate related lawsuits and actions in our courts. I find visiting this site regularly to be invaluable; it allows one to know what other agents do not.

Here are a few quick stories of what has happened to some of my sellers and how my contract knowledge made these issues easy to deal with.

STORY 1 - Every buyer does a final walkthrough of the home just prior to closing. They are looking for any major material differences, like the appliances being gone. In this instance, the buyer and his agent arrived at the closing and they passed me in the hall on their way in. I asked the buyer agent how the walkthrough went and he said that it had been great and that only a few minor repairs were needed. He handed me the document with the details. As I reviewed it, I quickly saw that they were asking for items that were no longer covered by the new real estate laws. Basically, the law had changed the previous July and he was either not aware of it or trying to pull one over on me and my seller.

I had a copy of the contract and I politely asked the agent to talk with me in another office while our clients were getting seated. I informed him that the contract area related to these items had changed and that the $2000 they were asking for to address these 'minor' repairs was not the obligation of the seller. He was shocked, and I suggested that he ask the real estate attorney directly – but privately – to avoid any hostility at the closing table. He and the attorney came back to the closing table ten minutes later and the agent leaned over and talked to his buyer. I found out later that he basically played it up as if he was going to be the big man and cover these costs for his buyer. He got caught not knowing his job or the contract, and to avoid his buyer wanting to walk out and being in default, he paid the $2000 knowing we would not.

My seller knew nothing about this going on until after all the papers were signed and we were done. He asked as we left what all the side meetings were about and I told him. He was very thankful for my knowledge of the contract and for saving him that $2000. By the way, that buyer agent was a part-time agent that up until that point had only closed 23 sales in his entire career. If I had also been part time and inexperienced, my seller would have lost the $2000 and potentially other money earlier in the sale.

STORY 2 – After months of negotiating a short sale for my seller, we finally had an approval to close. My seller was handicapped and needed to move out of the area for better medical treatment and therapy, so this closing was very important to her for many reasons. She would not be able to start her treatments until the home was sold.

As the days passed, we were getting very rude replies from the buyer's lender when we did our regular follow-up on the progress of the buyer's loan. This made me very cautious and I shared my concerns with the buyer agent. He assured me that everything was fine.

The next few weeks were about the same but we seemed to be moving forward. On the closing day, I woke up to an email that had come to my personal email address from the buyer agent. How he had that email address I wasn't sure, but the general content was this: "Hi Steve, so sorry but my buyer will not be able to close today, or at all, on this home. I'll call you later to explain."

I had been reading the email on my phone and now I literally ran to my laptop. I opened the contract, checked a few things and experienced a certain amount of relief. Next I called my seller and said that I had some troubling news but I was hopeful we could straighten it out. I explained her options and asked how she would like me to proceed. She chose the direction I had suggested.

Next I called the buyer agent and thankfully he answered. He apologized for the 'inconvenience' as he called it. I said "Well, Mr. Buyer Agent, (name changed to protect the uninformed) I spoke with my seller, and she and I will be closing at 4 pm as scheduled. If your buyer is unable to attend, please inform her she will be in default. Per the contract, the seller will be keeping her $10,000 escrow down payment and she will pursue the buyer in court for further damages." I was very calm and I restated that I was only sharing what the outcome would be if his buyer was unable to close. He then got hostile and said his buyer was voiding on financing, and since they had never removed this contingency, the buyer could now do that.

That was when the fun started for me. First, during the contract to closing phase, I had already shared with my seller that buyer agents often will try to keep from sending this in. Their hope is to do exactly what this agent was trying to do. But my seller was okay with that and we allowed that to be the case.

Here are the details of what I shared with the buyer agent – because there was a major flaw in his tactic.

1. Per our current contract at that time, all contingencies that were not previously removed, including financing, would be removed automatically at 12:01 a.m. the day of closing. So, his using the financing contingency as a way out was invalid. I even shared on what page and paragraph he could find that information in the contract. There was dead silence on the other end of the phone.

2. Additionally, per the contract, to use this way out, he was required to deliver to us a written notice signed by his buyer, along with a lender's denial letter, even if it were a valid option, which it was not. He did not do this.

3. Per the contract, all notices were to go to my work email address included in the contract to be considered 'delivered,' but he had sent it to my personal email address, which was not listed in the contract. But no matter, his method of trying to void was not applicable at all.

He was yelling at me and telling me I was a horrible agent to do this to his client. I reminded him that our job is to protect our own client, not the other agent's client. In the end, his buyer closed on the sale, albeit two weeks later. We found out later that the buyer wanted the home 100% but that at the last minute the lender referred to her by her agent told her the interest rate would be a full percent higher than originally quoted to her. When she heard that, she told them she wouldn't close at that rate. She found a new lender, closed, and is very happy with her new home.

If I had not known the contract as well as I did, my seller would have lost that closing, and due to it being a short sale, she possibly could have later lost the home to a foreclosure. The buyer would also have lost a home that she wanted but felt pressured to abandon based on the sudden and unexpected change in her interest rate.

Agents gain knowledge through effort and experience. They must actively study the various types of contracts and continue learning by going to continuing education and legal updates classes. Also, the more closings your agent has completed, the more prepared and informed they are to defend your best interests.

Select a Listing Specialist, not a Buyer Specialist

In the real estate game, the overwhelming majority of agents specialize in working with buyers. Why? Quite honestly, because it is much easier to sign a buyer as a client. Being confident, competent and able to prove your value to a seller is not something most agents do well. Personally, I am a Listing Specialist; I specialize in working for sellers. This specialization has enabled me to focus on and employ the best techniques for getting homes SOLD. When choosing the right agent to sell your home, you want to select a Listing Specialist. The unique benefit of being a Listing Specialist is that the buyers often come to you to find a home. It will be the same with the agent you choose, assuming you find a true Listing Agent.

How do you tell if your agent is a Listing Agent versus a Buyer Agent trying to help you sell your home? It starts with asking them what percentage of their annual sales comes from listings versus buyers. You want an answer of 80% or more for the listing side. But it only begins there. In my next chapter I will detail 11 highly important questions to ask the agents that you interview.

5
Eleven Probing Interview Questions for REALTORS®

It is crazy that some people spend more time and energy deciding where to go to dinner than they do selecting their Listing Agent. I see it all the time as I meet with sellers who did not sell, and as I review listings in the MLS by part-time agents with horrible photos, few details and zero marketing online anywhere. Put the time into asking your potential listing agent some critical and tough questions, and you will dramatically improve your odds of having a great experience – actually selling your home as well as getting the most money in your pocket at the end.

1) How long have you been licensed as a REALTOR?
Look for 10+ years. New agents or agents that are averaging less than four closings a year are far too inexperienced to help you properly.

2) Are you full time and have you been full time the whole time?

Of course, you want to hear a 'yes' here. You do not want a part-time agent. Also, try to find out if they have ever taken a break from real estate during that time. So many agents start, don't do well, put their license on hold for years, and then come back years later to try again. If they took a break, how long has their recent re-entry into real estate been going on?

3) Do you only work in real estate?

Some agents say they are full time even if they have a second job. They are trained to say they are dual-career. You want an agent who is *completely* focused on real estate only. You don't want, for example, a teacher that also happens to sell real estate.

4) How many homes have you sold to date?

This is an important question. Agents with a higher number of sales are better prepared to manage the hiccups and challenges that ultimately pop up along the way. The more homes they have dealt with and the more sales they have made, the better they will be able to support you in selling your home and the more they can keep you from losing money along the way. If possible, you are hoping to hear a number in the hundreds, possibly 300+. Personally, I would avoid the mega clearinghouse teams that do thousands, as you aren't dealing with the main agent and they seldom come to the closing with you.

5) What is the average number of days it takes to sell a home in my area, and how long does it take *you*

compared to those agents?

If homes in your area normally sell in an average of 45 days, you want your agent to have an average much lower than that. If they are successful as a Listing Agent, their average time on the market will always be better than the 'average' agent.

6) Are you a real estate <u>broker</u> or just an <u>agent</u>?

You want a Broker (Principal Broker or Associate Broker), not just an agent. To become a broker, there is a higher set of standards, more classroom time and additional testing.

7) What percentage of your sales are listings?

You want an agent that does over 80% of their business representing *sellers* versus buyers. This is the definition of a Listing Agent. They will be more versed in marketing your home, helping you price and prepare for the sale, and managing the details of the contract.

8) Can you show me your marketing plan for my home?

You are looking for a printed or digital copy of a specific marketing plan. Review it and compare it to what other agents are offering you. Successful agents *always* have a written plan of action.

9) Are you a 5-Star Premier Agent for Zillow?

Most REALTORs have a love/hate relationship with Zillow. But Zillow is now the #1 real estate portal on the web. Premier Agents pay money to Zillow (a monthly fee) to hold the Premier Agent status, and Premier Agents on Zillow can do more with their listings for their sellers than non-

Premier Agents. The 5-Star status is related to their online customer reviews on the site. A 5-Star (4.5-5) agent continues to show that they are producing at a high level and finishing sales with the sellers being highly satisfied with the work the agent has provided.

10) Who takes the photos of my home for the Internet?

Do not hire an agent that takes their own photos. They may say they know better what buyers want to see, but what that really means is that they don't want to spend the money on professional photos for your home, or that they just don't have the money. You only want an agent that hires a professional photographer every time for every home. The difference in quality is remarkable. Every day as I look through the MLS listings, I get angry at these agents that are letting their clients down. The photos and details they place in their listings are at such an amateur level that it is embarrassing to call them REALTORS®.

11) What % of the asking price do you average on your listings?

If the agent isn't over 98%, I would reconsider hiring them. It means they either priced too high at the start, which suggests they don't know the market, or they priced high to get the seller to sign the listing papers.

However, these 11 questions should never override your natural intuition. If something just doesn't feel right, then move on and talk with other agents.

If you want the right to demand a high level of service and results, you need to step up and do a better job interviewing the person that will help you manage the sale of your high value property. For most of us, it is the most expensive investment we have. Don't hand it over to a part-time, inexperienced REALTOR® because you're too busy to sit down and ask the important questions.

6
Getting Your Home Ready for the Market

Getting your property ready for the market begins with an honest assessment of your property's current condition. The way your home looked while you lived in it and enjoyed it may be very different from how your home will look during the selling process. If my clients will be occupying the home during the selling process, I try to strike that delicate balance between homeowner comfort and stellar showcasing.

In my opinion, the single most important thing you can do in the preparation process is to de-clutter your home. If needed, rent a local storage space versus using your basement, spare bedroom or garage. Once your home is de-cluttered, the next two items are cleaning and painting. These three things will not cost very much or take much time, but you will be surprised by the difference they will make.

Tip: *Almost all storage places will offer one month of storage for free or for $1. Look for these offers and if you don't find one, simply ask when you call. I've done this many times and it helps to reduce your storage costs.*

1. **De-clutter**. When you think about the idea of de-cluttering, think of floor space and counter space. Generally, you will want to display the maximum amount of floor space and the maximum amount of countertop. As you look around at the floors and counter spaces (including tabletops, desks, etc.) of your home, identify things that don't belong and make these areas as clear as possible. If you have large pieces of furniture that are taking up a big chunk of floor space and can be eliminated, consider putting those items in storage or selling them if you won't need them in your next home. The more uncluttered floor space the buyer can see, the larger and more inviting your home will feel.

2. **Clean**. A good deep clean is an absolute necessity after you have removed the clutter. This involves cleaning your home both inside and out. The floors, walls, baseboards, doors, and all surfaces in your home should be thoroughly cleaned. If possible, the outside of your home and the driveways and walkways should be power washed. When it comes to cleaning, I recommend that you either form a cleaning crew (you and three or more friends), or better yet, simply hire a cleaning service. A good deep clean should cost around $200-$350 or so, depending on the size and condition of your home. For the power washing, I recommend you hire a reputable contractor. I lost a good set of window screens to hiring a neighbor's son who used their power washer. He destroyed three screens before realizing he had the pressure

too high for use on the screens. We both learned a valuable lesson there but at my expense.

3. **Paint**. Once your home is de-cluttered and clean, it's time to paint! Take a good look at all of the walls, baseboards, doors, window sills and ceilings around your home. In some cases they will just need to be touched up here and there; other areas will need to be entirely repainted. Be objective and make a list. Then decide whether or not you will do the work yourself or hire someone. Paint is probably the least expensive way to make a dramatic improvement to your home. Neutral colors are key. Paint over that bright red wall in your kitchen, or that outdated mustard yellow in your living room. You will want to appeal to the majority of buyers and neutral colors are the way to accomplish this.

Home Repairs

I strongly encourage sellers to complete any minor and cosmetic home repairs that you can afford to do. This includes addressing things like broken light fixtures or switches, burned out light bulbs, torn screens, wood rot, cracked caulking, broken tiles, leaking faucets, cracked windows, broken wall plates (outlets and switches), loose doorknobs, etc.

While you and your family may have been perfectly content to live with these minor items, they are a red flag to prospective home buyers. Home buyers generally suspect that homes with small items in disrepair will likely have bigger items that have not been addressed.

It's easy to compile a list of things that need to be done and then pay a handyman to complete your list of minor repairs in less than a day. A reliable source online can be HomeAdvisor.com or Angie's List where past clients rate each contractor.

What if you can't afford to do the repairs? No worries. Consider using an "As-Is" pricing strategy, and talk with your chosen listing agent on how this will impact your sale.

Tip: Looking around, you may be able to find a contractor that will do all the work you need and wait to be paid until you close on the sale of your home. This is a bit riskier for both parties but I have seen it done successfully many times. If your home needs that much work, it may be worth investigating.

Digging Deeper (Getting a Pre-Inspection)

For sellers who want to go one step further, a pre-sale home inspection can be considered. The cost is typically around $300 to $400, and the inspector will give you a written report of what was found. Then you can select the major items and correct them.

My experience shows that buyers will always ask for two to five times the estimated cost for a repair. They do this because they worry that something else will be found during the repair. Also, they consider it an inconvenience and they feel they should be compensated for it. Avoid these losses by taking control up front. A word of caution though: the buyer will still hire their own inspector and their inspection may show other items needing attention.

Staging

While de-cluttering, cleaning, painting and minor repairs will *prepare* your home for sale, staging is the process of *showcasing* your home for sale. Do we really need HGTV to show us over and over again how impactful a staged home is to a buyer? The positive impact of staging has been totally proven.

Homeowners can try to tackle staging themselves but too often this is glossed over. Here's an overview of what you should focus on.

- Color: Use warm and soothing colors to paint your home. Lighter shades are more attractive to the eye and they help buyers to visualize their household items in the home.
- Maintenance: Make your house look and smell clean. In addition, try to complete any home improvement project you are carrying out on your property.
- De-personalizing and De-cluttering: Take your personal stuff out of the house. Otherwise, it will distract home buyers during their property inspection.
- Emotional Cues: Help buyers to emotionally connect with your home by decorating it with candles and flowers.
- Furniture Placement: Place minimal furniture in your home to showcase the large space to potential buyers.

If you are feeling overwhelmed, consider hiring a professional staging company. There is an expense, but this investment will be returned with a higher offer price, shorter days on the market, and excited buyers that want your home enough to overlook any minor flaws.

A seller asked me once, during a particularly hot seller market, why they should bother staging their home. They felt that if it was clean, it would quickly get an offer. I asked if they would like more money than they expected for their home. They said "Yes, of course." I asked if they wanted buyers to fight over their home with multiple offers. They said yes again. I said "Then stage it." They did, and they received not only one of the highest offers in that neighborhood during that period of time but also multiple offers!

Staging is also the finishing touch that takes the professional photos to the next level. The quality of the photos that make it online are the foundation for the interest in your home compared to others, and for all the marketing created by your agent. Staging prior to professional photos is a slam dunk when compared to your neighbors who are also selling.

Doubt any of this even a little? Go onto Pinterest or any of your favorite social media sites and search for before-and-after staging photographs. If you are not floored by these transformations, I would be very surprised.

The average cost to have a professional staging person come into your home and provide you with a written report of what you can do on your own is about $400-500. The cost for them to come in and stage your home with their furniture is typically around 1% of the listing price of your home, but it can run up to 3% depending on the size of your home and what the staging requires. Often the added cost is when the staging and furniture rental is for a period of time, say 30 days. Typically, this only includes main living spaces, but they can stage other rooms for a slight add-on to that fee.

Statistics from the National Association of Realtors (NAR) show that the cost of staging can be 1 to 3% of the listing price, with a return on your investment of 8 to 10%. Add to that the fact that your home will receive an offer an average of 73% faster than an un-staged home. There are also other related financial benefits to a staged home. Selling faster saves you additional mortgage, utility and association fees.

Overall, the results are in and have been tested over and over. A professionally staged home sells faster and for more money than homes that are not staged.

The Emotion of Buying

The most important single reason that a home sells is its Emotional Appeal. Over 90% of buyers in today's market buy on emotion. Looking at your house through 'a buyer's eyes' can help you prepare your home to sell for the best price in the least amount of time. When you begin preparing your home, begin outside and work your way in. Make up a "to do" list as you go along, keeping in mind the importance of first impressions. If you have already hired a REALTOR® they will help you put this list together.

EXTERIOR TIPS

If I shared how many times a buyer has said "no, keep driving" as we pulled up to a home, I could fill another book. The impact of your exterior curb appeal is immediate, and many buyers will not even bother getting out of the car if the curb appeal isn't there.

Clean up the exterior, cut back bushes, trim trees, remove trash, power wash, replace rotted wood, paint where needed, and replace broken screens and damaged siding. Keep your lawn cut and clear of debris. Paint your front door, consider updating your front door handle, and make the entry shine. Doors are a main focal point so make them beautiful.

Also, add some new plants or planters and even some inexpensive solar lighting to really dress up your entry.

Let's be honest: you already know what needs to be done, but it can seem overwhelming. Hire some local workers, or kids, or the boy or girl scouts to come out and help.

If you have dogs, like I do, make sure you have picked up after your pets in your yard. You sure don't want a buyer having a bad experience when walking around the outside of your home (and then inside – ewww).

INTERIOR TIPS

When showing your home to prospective buyers, you want to make everything look spacious, organized, bright, warm, and welcoming. Start with a full housecleaning from top to bottom. A clean home will sell a lot faster than a dirty one.

For closets, empty out one-third of what is hanging, clear the floor completely, and neatly organize all items on the shelves. It is important to show *space* in the closet.

For tabletops and end tables, there should be no more than two or three items on any table. Put all items on the kitchen counters away and out of sight.

Remove your area rugs and show off the floors. Area rugs always make a room look smaller. Yes, they are great for catching stuff under dining spaces, but they do a horrible job of showing off the space in your home. When in doubt, just remove them.

KITCHEN & BATHROOM TIPS

Kitchens sell homes. Please read that again! **Kitchens sell homes!** If there is only one place in your home you can afford to focus on, it should be the kitchen. At a minimum, consider updating cabinet hardware, faucets and appliances. Sand and repaint cabinets if you cannot afford to replace them. Add that backsplash that you always wanted to add but never did. Flooring is key too and it should be new or exceptionally clean.

Bathrooms are also focal points for most buyers. Be sure they are clean and clear of clutter. Scrub the sinks and tubs and shower stalls and add new shower curtains. Remove old and decaying caulking and have it reapplied.

DECLUTTERING TIPS

Eliminating clutter will give your home a more spacious look. By removing or storing things you don't need, you can create a roomy, comfortable feeling that will be inviting to prospective buyers. If a house is too cluttered, buyers have trouble imagining themselves and their belongings in it. Remember: when in doubt, move it out!

CLEANING TIPS

When a home is clean, it gives the impression that it has been well cared for. Wipe off those dusty ceiling fan blades and light fixtures, and light bulbs too.

If you have a two-story foyer or living room, you must get help to clean those window ledges and shelves. As of my writing this book, I have had two separate buyers talk about dirty ledges that are out of reach. Be safe, hire someone if you must, but get them cleaned.

This brings me to plants, specifically plastic ones. Get rid of any plastic plants and replace them with live ones. Plastic plants are typically coated in dust and distract from the attractiveness of your home. Do not neglect your live plants. Dust their leaves, remove discolored leaves to spruce up their appearance.

REPAIRING TIPS

Call it the honey-do list, your to-do list, or your never-got-to-it list. Now is the time to address all those minor repairs that you have been putting off.

Fix that sticking door, replace those air filters, and as for that window that won't open…guess what? Yep, you should get that fixed too. These repairs may seem annoying and trivial, but not fixing them will add up to big money requests from a buyer that decides to make you an offer. Or worse, they may keep buyers from making an offer at all.

NEUTRALIZING

Creating a neutral atmosphere in your home has a positive impact on selling. Add neutral paint, tone down those crazy sports-themed rooms, and get rid of the personal items in the home.

If you are a hunter, gun enthusiast or medal winning Olympian, now is not the time to highlight your passions. You will be moving soon, so pack up your trophies and pictures and neutralize your home to sell it faster.

DON'T OVER-IMPROVE

I touched on this earlier. It is crazy how many times I walk into a home to find out they have just paid huge money for updates that won't give them a decent return or may even detract from their return. Remember that a real estate agent is there to help you make the right decisions based on your current home selling market.

Remember that the Kitchen, Master Bedroom and Bathrooms are the most important rooms. If your home needs some attention, focus first on these rooms.

7
Pricing Your Home to Sell Not Sit

All I do, all day long, every day, is look at homes in the local market. I'm watching the trends and keeping an eye out for those homes that aren't selling. What I have learned over my years in this business is that setting a listing price for a home is as much an art form as it is facts and figures. Get five real estate agents in the same room and you could end up with five different values for your home. This is another reason why it is so important to *qualify* the agent that you are thinking of hiring. You won't hire them based on what they say your home is worth. You will hire them based on their experience and their qualifications. Then, working with your REALTOR®, you will set a price based on the facts, the figures, your goals, and your real estate agent's assessment of the market trends.

It is also important to know that pricing can become a moving target based on what is happening in your market. A price that felt perfect one day may feel too high two weeks later. Your agent will examine the facts of record to determine the most effective pricing strategy to help you obtain the maximum price. It is so important for your agent to understand what the market is doing and how the market is currently trending (shifting up, down, or staying flat).

How Price is Determined

Price is determined by <u>what a buyer is willing to pay</u> for a home. Ultimately, at the end of the day, the market price is set by the buyer. Therefore, it is critical for your agent to dig around and discover exactly what buyers are currently paying for a home as like yours as possible.

The agent you select should be able to show you all the data they use to determine what buyers are currently willing to pay for a home like yours. Also, by showing you the market trends in your neighborhood, the agent can determine whether it makes more sense to sell now or possibly to wait. This is another area where choosing the wrong agent can cause your sale great harm. Choose wisely.

Getting a CMA (Comparative Market Analysis)

A CMA is an extremely helpful tool that REALTORS® use to determine what the market is saying. The CMA is a side-by-side comparison report of homes currently for sale and homes that have SOLD in the same neighborhood or area as yours. Typically, it includes new listings (for sale), pending sales (under contract), closed sales (solds), and expired listings (failed to sell).

CMAs can vary widely, depending on the knowledge, skill level and experience of the agent inputting the search parameters, as well as the data fields that are chosen. This is a delicate and critical job that will help you achieve maximum success, and you do not want to get this information from the wrong agent. I still meet agents that have been licensed a long time but have not closed many transactions, and they constantly need help trying to calculate the value of a seller's home they are placing on the market.

You also don't want to trust an online source that spits out un-scrubbed and unverified data. While we are discussing it, the 'Z-esti-muliate' (changed to protect the innocent) provided by one of the real estate portals out there is typically far from what the 'market' value is in our area. So work with your agent to determine the true value, or you may lose tens of thousands of dollars in the process.

Select an agent who is intimately familiar with your local area and neighborhoods. This puts them in the best position to help educate you on what the market is doing, how the market is trending, and how to get the most for your home in the least amount of time.

LOCATION

One thing you may have heard about real estate is that the top three factors in home value are location, location, location. For example, a home in Arlington may sell for $200k more than a similar home in Haymarket, Virginia. It's all about location.

When building your CMA, the agent must use comparables from your neighborhood, not from areas far outside of it. They should also pull a report of every home that has SOLD on your street in the past year so they can find trending data.

SIZE

Generally speaking, they should try to keep the comparable properties to within 10% of the size of your home.

AGE

When aggregating the data, they should select comparables that were built the exact same year as your home or within five years plus or minus.

OTHER DETAILS

There are quite a few other parameters that are considered to get the most accurate results, including the number of bedrooms, bathrooms, garage spaces, living areas, the number of stories, and more.

REVIEW OF EACH COMPARABLE

After your agent compiles the data, they need to go through every comparable property and review the photographs and property descriptions. This exercise helps them better drill down and select the best comparables. When possible, they should drive through your neighborhood and make a visual analysis of the comparables, and get inside them if possible.

ANALYZING THE DATA

Once the CMA is completed, the next step is for you and your agent to analyze and review the data together.

Once the agent has analyzed all the data and made a visual inspection of your property, they can look at the critical step of setting your price.

Pricing Strategy Meeting

Although most sellers expect the agent to tell them what they think the price of their home should be, I believe that the agent's role is to educate their clients on what the market is doing in their area. Unlike most REALTORS®, I don't engage in a discussion of listing price with homeowners until they have hired me. Why? Quite simply, it is one of the values I bring to the table over other agents. I will discuss a value range and estimated time to sell. But the discussion regarding actual value and my suggestion of a listing price does not happen until we sit down to go over the information together.

I call this my Pricing Strategy Meeting. It is also the time when I need to have the hard discussion with a seller who thinks their Viking stove means a $20,000 higher listing price for their house when compared to the exact same model that sold the week before without one.

The seller chooses the listing price based on the information that the real estate agent shared with them. The buyer then decides if that price fits what the home is offering. Remember that, as the seller, you have the final say to any offers. Yes, the buyer sets the market value by what they are willing to offer, but you get to say NO or counter their initial offer. Therefore, I remind sellers to price *at* and not *above* the market value. Sellers may say they want to create 'negotiating' room, but being priced too high keeps buyers away. Price properly, and remember you are never obligated to accept any offer if you do not like the bottom-line.

BUILDING IN NEGOTIATING ROOM

One of the most common and critical mistakes a seller makes when pricing their home is trying to build in negotiating room. They want to make certain that when all the negotiating is done, they get their price. That is a HUGE MISTAKE.

When a seller does this, they price themselves out of the market that is looking for their home. Buyers that do come to the home expect more from the home, based on that inflated price, so they are most often under-impressed and continue looking. Buyers will know you are priced high because of the homes they have already seen, and their buyer agent is going to confirm that as well. So buyers will just move on.

Sellers who build in negotiating room wonder where all the offers are. They think that a buyer should at least send them some type of offer to review, but it never arrives. They ask: shouldn't the buyer at least send in a lower offer if that is what they think it is worth? The answer again is no. My experience shows that time and time again the would-be buyer just completely moves on.

Here is what I tell my sellers, and it works all the time. Price *at* the market, not *above* it. Do not buffer your price to allow for negotiation. Why? Very simply because they, the sellers, always have the final say on accepting any offer. If an offer comes in low, simply counter the offer to a price you will accept or just say no!

Pricing high also seriously extends your days on the market, and many buyers, after seeing that home on the market for a long period without selling, assume something is wrong with the home. So this adds another reason they never come out to see it.

Other Pricing Factors To Be Aware Of

THE BUYER'S APPRAISAL

It is important to understand that most buyers will be using some form of financing when they purchase your home. This means that the buyer's lender will order an appraisal on your property. If the home does not appraise for at least the amount of the sale price, the buyer's loan can be rejected. The buyer now can void the offer, negotiate a lower offer or even bring additional cash to make up that difference if they want the home. Guess which one they usually go for? Yes, the one that has you reducing your price.

If your agent can articulate and prove your listing value by sharing data, amenities and upgrades that can easily be overlooked, you may be able to get that value adjusted. Be prepared, though, because getting any appraiser to change their value is extremely challenging.

BUYER'S MARKET VS. SELLER'S MARKET

Simply put, in a buyer's market there are more homes than there are buyers, and in a seller's market there are fewer homes than there are buyers.

HOW PRICING IMPACTS SHOWINGS

Research has proven that price drives traffic to a listing, and that pricing a property correctly at the beginning of the listing process will attract the most potential buyers to your home. Fewer visits results in fewer opportunities to receive a contract.

PRICING UNIQUE AND LUXURY PROPERTIES

For homes that are rare or unique, it is often recommended that you order an appraisal by a licensed appraiser. While your agent may actually use the same criteria, software and systems as most appraisers, the appraiser will be seen by the buyer and the buyer's lender as a very credible source when it is difficult to clearly see the value of your property. I suggest this strategy for unique properties with recent upgrades or large acreage properties, and also for the luxury inventory line (homes priced at $1.5 Million+).

AS-IS PRICING

The "As-Is" pricing strategy is for sellers who lack the funds, ability or desire to properly prepare their home for sale. This strategy is often paired with the seller getting a home inspection prior to setting the list price or placing the home on the market for sale. After reviewing the potential costs for repair, the list price is adjusted accordingly to allow for this value loss. Often an even greater value is deducted due to the buyer's concern regarding unforeseen issues and the inconvenience of needing to do repairs prior to occupying the home.

If the repairs needed are significant, it is possible that the buyer will be unable to get a loan to purchase the home. When this happens, you need cash-only buyers and the value is often reduced even more.

THE FIRST 7 WEEKS

The best chance for selling your property is within the first seven weeks. Studies show that the longer a property stays on the market, the less the seller will net, so make certain you price it right.

It is very important to price your property at a competitive market value at the signing of the listing agreement. The market is so competitive that even overpricing by a few thousand dollars could mean that your house will have difficulty selling.

8
Marketing Your Home for Sale

In the past few years, computers and the Internet have completely changed the face of real estate, and unfortunately most agents haven't kept up. According to the recent study by the National Association of REALTORS® (NAR), 90+% of all home buyers use the Internet for house hunting. Knowing this, isn't it crazy to hear that most REALTORS® you meet have no idea how to successfully market your home to today's Internet-savvy home buyers? I speak with agents every day and I can share that less than 10% of them have ever placed a marketing advertisement for a home they are selling onto a social media platform like Facebook, Instagram, Pinterest, YouTube or Snapchat. That, in my mind, is borderline malpractice. While you, the seller, don't need to know how to do this, there is no denying the power of marketing online and specifically within social media. I don't mean adding pictures of your home to their business accounts on these platforms. I'm speaking of paid advertising that targets home buyers locally and internationally that would be interested in your home.

Besides not staying up to date with technology, less than 9% of agents are trained in the fine art of sales and marketing. That's because sales and marketing is *not* included in the training that agents receive in order to become licensed. The truth is that most agents are good people; they just don't know how to do good marketing. Doing the kind of marketing that leads to a successful sale takes time, money and a carefully designed marketing plan.

The average agent only uses the 3-P's marketing plan:

1. **P**ut a sign in the yard
2. **P**ut the home in the MLS
3. **P**ray that it will sell!

Now let me share what a comprehensive marketing plan includes. Look for an agent that provides ALL the strategies listed below. If they do not, ask them why. Typically, you will hear some excuse: that only works in some areas, or it's really just a tool to get sellers to sign listing papers and it doesn't really work. I would challenge those responses with the following: If you are trying to sell a home and knowing that a potential buyer can come from so many different places, why would you not pull out *all* the stops immediately, even if this generated only one buyer lead? It only takes one right buyer to get your home sold. Your agent should be aggressive and not be looking for ways to save themselves money in marketing expenses.

Marketing efforts should focus on three major categories

1) Photos, 3D Virtual Tours & Video; 2) On-site Advertising; and 3) Internet Advertising.

1 - Photos and 3D Virtual Tours

It all starts here! After your home is prepared and ready, your agent needs to step up and perform. Any successful marketing plan starts with the photos. I am shocked at how often I see listings in our MLS with poor photos or only a few pictures or even no pictures. Don't be that home online that everyone passes by.

☐ **Professional Photos** – The key here is *professional*. The difference between using a professional photographer and your agent taking them is night and day. Do *not* hire an agent that takes their own photos. Many do this because they don't have the money to hire a professional. Picture day is an event! It's scheduled, and you have homework the night before and the morning of. It can be cancelled at the last minute due to weather. But all this hard work is the *foundation* for your home's presence online. Additionally, most MLS systems allow for at least 30-35 high resolution photos to be uploaded. Your home better have as many as possible if it is going to compete with other homes in the area.

☐ **3D Virtual Tours** – This one is ignored by so many agents. Why? Because this costs them money. Great marketing starts with photos **and your tour**. It is not free, but your agent better be in a place to fund and get these done for you. In the old days, virtual tours were simply panoramic views – basically, multiple photos 'stitched' together that allowed you a wider view that you could 'pan' through from left to right or up and down. Now they are amazing 3D Walkthrough Tours that allow your viewer to actually 'walk' around a kitchen island and really experience the home almost as if they were in the home. Check out this sample: http://bit.ly/3dtoursample. Visit the page and click on the 3D link to view the 3D Walkthrough. Smaller homes often do not get the same benefits from a 3D Tour due to the tight spaces, but it is still worth investigating with your agent.

☐ **Video** – If pictures can sell your home, then how about video? Did you know that YouTube is now one of the largest search engines? Just behind its big brother Google. That's how important video has become. For video, there are a few different approaches out there:

- Agent walk-through video. This is where the agent films the home as they walk through it and talks about its great features. I like this approach because it's more personal and it connects with the viewer.

- Drone or professional fly-through. This is a professional drone pilot or videographer filming the interior of your home. An absolute must on larger, luxury homes.

- Aerial drone footage. A drone is used to take aerial

still photos and video. Perfect for larger homes and for homes with some land and great landscaping.

2 - On-site Advertising

☐ **Direct Dial Number.** Buyers can call and get instant information from a live person!

☐ **24 Hour Info Hotline!** Prospects can call 24 hours a day and get information on your home. When a buyer calls the number, your agent then receives a text notification that someone has called about your property. The text notification has the client's phone number, so your agent can call them back right away and schedule a showing! This is often called IVR (Instant Voice Response) or Text-to-Talk – ask your agent about it.

☐ **Full Color Virtual Flyers.** This ties into the 24/7 phone number, or sometimes it's done separately with a QR code (Quick Response). When they call the number, or scan the QR code with their smartphone, they are immediately sent a link to your home's photos, virtual tour and details, so buyers can pull up the up-to-date home information right there and even immediately connect with your agent.

3 - Internet Advertising

☐ **Brokerage Websites & National Portals.** I will

touch on this in detail in my Bonus Chapter on REALTOR® Lies and Misdirection, but it's safe to say that ANY agent that enters your home into the local MLS system will, by default, have your home appear on every major brokerage website. This means that your home will be featured on sites like Keller Williams, RE/MAX, Coldwell Banker, and all the local mom-and-pop real estate outfits as well. So even though you list with them, your home will be featured on just about every other brokerage site in town and throughout the nation. Your home will also be included on popular websites like Zillow, Trulia and REALTOR.com. Make no mistake; the MLS and the Brokerage do this, not your agent!

☐ **Craigslist.** Do not dismiss the power of Craigslist. It doesn't matter if your home is under $100,000 or well into the millions; Craigslist continues to produce buyer leads. Possibly it's the simplicity of the site and the lack of advertisement clutter that draws people to it. An agent that includes Craigslist as a regular part of their marketing can generate a steady stream of buyer inquiries every day.

☐ **Social Media.** As mentioned earlier, the use of Facebook, Instagram, YouTube and many other popular social media platforms to market your property is critical. It's not your agent posting your home details to their personal or business accounts that does anything at all. It is their PAYING for advertisements and TARGETING HOME BUYERS using those platforms that is important.

9
Showing Your Home

OK – now that your home is on the market, it is time to move forward and get it SOLD!

It is important to make your home as easy to show as possible. If your home is vacant, this will obviously be easy, since buyers can go without notice and you don't have to prep for every showing. If your home is occupied, however, providing buyers with a hassle-free showing process will require a bit more work.

Keep in mind that when buyers are out looking at properties, they may be viewing several homes that day. That's because most buyers view homes in "batches" (three today in your area and four tomorrow in another area). If they are asking to view your home at a particular time, it usually means that they will be in your area within that timeframe. If you do not allow your home to be one of the properties viewed, it may be eliminated from their list.

This is why I always recommend, although it may be inconvenient, that you allow your home to be viewed (and be prepped for viewings) whenever possible and within reason.

If you have circumstances that do not allow you to leave your home quickly (you work from home, take care of an elderly parent or small children, etc.), special instructions can be placed in the MLS, like "seller requests 2 hours' notice prior to showing." Unless your home is particularly unique and desirable, I do not suggest you set your showings up by appointment only. Years in this profession have shown me that most agents are lazy. When an appointment is required and they have other homes to show, they often remove the 'by appointment' homes from their showing list with the thought of coming back later. So, they may come back if they don't find anything else first, or they may never come back at all.

Showing with Renters in Your Home

Homes that are currently rented create a new set of challenges when it comes to showing. Tenants are often uncomfortable about the idea of allowing the home to be shown and can make the showing process more difficult. If buyers are having a difficult time getting in to see the property, you will have a difficult time getting it sold.

My advice is to enlist the cooperation of your tenants. Try to offer them some kind of incentive for cooperating during the showing process. Perhaps you can give them $20 off their rent for every showing, or something creative like that. Getting them onboard is critical. If they are *not* onboard, it might be worth waiting for them to leave before trying to sell.

Another challenge to showing a tenant-occupied property is that the tenants will likely not have the home in "show" condition because they are not personally vested in the successful sale of the property. In some cases, they could even be working *against* you if selling the home has a negative impact on their moving timeframe. Again, my advice is to seek the cooperation of your tenant. Give them a list of tips for showing the house and offer them an incentive for their cooperation.

My Top Tips on Showing Your Home

When it's time for a buyer's agent to show your home, all your preparations will be worth the effort. Here are a few final tips that can add that extra touch.

- Make sure not to be in the house when they are inside. Also, avoid lingering just outside, as buyers will be uncomfortable and will rush their viewing time in your home.
- Do not engage in questions with the buyer or buyer agent. The buyer agent's job is to find negotiating strength and the agent will often ask questions directed at finding out your weak spots. Additionally, most sellers share *too much*. They think they are 'selling' the home and its features but they end up putting doubt and concerns in the buyer's head. Direct all questions to your agent.
- Open the drapes and blinds. One exception might be the view. If the view from a particular window is bad,

keep the drapes closed, or at least don't open them completely.
- Turn on all lights even during the day. Think about new home models. Have you noticed that even during the day the lights are on inside the home? There is a reason for that. It makes the interior of the home feel larger and of course brighter. Nobody wants a dark dreary home.
- No dishes in the sink; empty the dishwasher and keep all trashcans out of site. Place small appliances, coffee makers and such out of view.
- Put toys, including pet toys, away.
- Make all the beds.
- Check that all the bathrooms are clean
- Never let people in that are not with their Real Estate agent. Safety can be a concern.
- If you happen to be home, do not let the agent walk in without registering their visit by using the electronic lockbox that has been installed. If they have forgotten their access card, have them identify themselves properly.

10
Working With Offers

This is what it is all about. You have put your time in by finding the right agent; you have prepared your home; the marketing has been launched; and now you are looking at an offer. If you have done everything in chapter nine, you should be looking at a strong offer soon. Statistically speaking, the highest offer is almost always your first offer. But sometime, just sometimes, it can be your lowest.

Sellers and buyers are adversaries in this process but they shouldn't be. They both have the same objective. The seller wants to sell the home and the buyer wants to acquire it. This means that a successful sale achieves the goals of both parties. But let us face the facts: the best offer means nothing if there is no strength behind it and it never makes it to closing.

So, let me go over the process of receiving an offer and moving forward. Once offers on your home are received, it's a good idea for your agent to run a revised CMA, so you can see exactly what the market in your neighborhood is doing at the time the offer is received. Then you will review the offer together and discuss the pros and cons of the offer. Additionally, your agent should be skilled enough to complete and bring a *Seller's Estimated Net Sheet* for all offers. This is a worksheet that shows you what your net proceeds will be based on each offer submitted. After you have looked at all the information, you will be in a position to respond to the offer.

Reviewing the Offer

The first thing you should do is review the details of the offer, the price and the terms. Here are the main points of the offer/contract that your agent should review with you:

OFFER PRICE

For some sellers, this is the *only* important factor of an offer, but I'll share why others can also be major players when considering an offer or multiple offers. If the offer is at your asking price, then on the surface it's a good starting point. If it is low, don't panic just yet; review the rest of the terms with your agent and get a look at the big picture.

Part of the offer will also show whether the buyer is paying all cash or using a loan. If they are using a loan, how much cash they will be putting down is an important factor, especially when considering multiple offers.

FINANCING

Knowing how the buyer intends to structure their

financing and what type of loan they are approved for is very helpful. Of course, your agent should always verify that the buyer is pre-approved to purchase your property. If there is any question or doubt, even after you have received the pre-approval letter, your agent should contact the buyer's lender and ask critical questions that will validate that the buyer is creditworthy.

Also, what lender the buyer is using can be very important. An experienced listing agent will be able to share their concerns about the buyer using Acme Loan Services located in Hawaii versus a local and known lender. There have been many offers where we have asked the buyer to also get preapproved by a local lender we knew and trusted before we would accept their offer

Pre-approval letters are far from bullet proof. If there is an undiscovered credit issue found during the actual application process or underwriting, a deal can fall apart quickly. Your agent must stay in contact with the buyer's agent and lender throughout the process to hopefully hold off any last-minute surprises. If a deal is going to fall apart, the faster you know the better.

ESCROW

Here, the buyer is agreeing to deposit what some call 'earnest money.' This amount is held in escrow by the title company, escrow company, buyer agent's brokerage, or the attorney that will close the transaction. The earnest money also gives you some security if the buyer defaults on the deal. There may be some exceptions to this rule, and if there is, your agent will discuss with you in greater detail.

CLOSING

The contract also contains the proposed closing date. Most closing dates are set for 30 to 45 days out. When reviewing the offer, discuss whether the proposed closing date works for you. The closing date can be an important part of the offer. I have had sellers select a lower offer simply because the buyer with the highest offer needed a 60-day closing and the sellers just could not wait that long. For them, the lower offer worked best and they selected it and closed 30 days later.

CLOSING COSTS

On every transaction, the seller has their own closing costs (sales compensation, title policy, escrow costs, recording fees, etc.), and the buyer has their closing costs (loan origination, prepaid expenses, insurance, title insurance, etc.). Also, it is not uncommon for the buyer to ask the seller to pay some or all their closing costs when putting an offer together.

Rather than focusing on the amount the buyer is asking you to pay on their behalf, it is better to focus on your 'net offer.' Your net offer is the sales price offered less buyer requested credits. For example, let's say you are asking $450,000 for your home and you receive an offer of $445,000 and the buyer requests a credit amount of $5,000. So, the net offer is $440,000. Your agent will help you navigate through all this and help you make the right decision for your selling goals. Most important: if you have an experienced listing agent, they will have already prepared a seller net sheet for your review.

SELLER'S ESTIMATED NET SHEET

Your listing agent should be well versed in completing and providing you with a seller's net sheet. It shows you the estimated amount you will net at closing after all costs and based on the offer submitted. This helps you make an informed decision when accepting or countering offers.

RECEIVING MULTIPLE OFFERS

Receiving multiple offers can be a blessing but must be handled carefully. When more than one offer is received on your home, your agent will generally contact all agents and let them know that multiple offers have been received; and they will most likely ask the buyer agents to invite their clients to counter with their highest and best offer. This strategy can sometimes generate offers that are above your list price! However, as I mentioned before, if we accept an offer that is outside the range of what the home will be appraised for, the buyer may have difficulty getting a loan, if a loan is part of the offer being considered.

Always bear in mind that multiple offers can backfire and send skittish buyers heading for the hills. The situation has to be handled very professionally, and often coaching is needed for the buyers' agents throughout the process.

A good agent will also try to get the buyer with the *second* strongest offer to consider it as a signed backup offer to the first. What this means is: if the first buyer flakes out or isn't able to close, you will already have an offer waiting in the background to get you to closing, without having to place your home back onto the market. However, it is important to know that the second position buyer can continue to look for a home, and if they find one they like, they can void their backup offer at any time and without penalty.

LOWBALL OFFERS

It is perfectly normal and common to become emotionally upset when you receive an offer that is far below what you consider to be 'acceptable.' However, my advice is to take a step back and take another look at the situation. Don't be upset with the buyer who made an offer. Instead, be upset with all the people who have looked at your home and didn't bother to make an offer. A low offer is simply an invitation to negotiate.

NEGOTIATION IS AN ART FORM

Negotiation is an art form. When negotiating your deal, the goal is to work to achieve your goals while trying to ensure that the buyer feels they are also getting a fair shake.

Sometimes negotiation will involve getting the buyer to see beyond dollars and cents. It is quite possible that the buyer's agent did a poor job of advising their client of your home's true value. If an offer is low, your agent should emphasize to the buyer agent the features of your home and why it's worth what you are asking. Many times, the other agent is new, part-time or inexperienced. So, if you provide additional details during the counter offer phase, it gives the buyer agent the facts they need to help support your counter and puts them in a position to actually help you get the number you want.

INSPECTIONS

Buyers have quite a few inspections they can initiate when buying a home. In Virginia, it really is a buyer-beware state. It is up to a buyer to do their due diligence before going to closing.

When you receive an offer, the inclusion or omission of inspections can definitely make or break a deal. In a hot seller's market, buyers may skip doing a home inspection. While this may sound great, sometimes this can backfire for a seller. Additional inspections, like for pests, well, septic, lead and radon, may also be requested. Your agent will discuss how the inspections or lack thereof may impact you. Weigh all of this into consideration when accepting or countering an offer that you have received.

11
Closing Your Sale

Now that your home is under contract, you can relax, but only a little. There are still a few things that can derail the transaction. At this critical juncture, your agent must remain diligent and do everything humanly possible to ensure a smooth closing for you. Often this means doing the job of the other agent. As has already been mentioned, many agents are either new or part time and do a very poor job. There is a fine line when it comes to keeping the transaction moving forward while never crossing the line of working for the buyer, and it takes a skilled agent to manage having a poor agent on the other side. Sadly, this is the situation in many closings, more than you would ever imagine.

The Buyer Inspection Process

Once your home is under contract, the buyer will typically order a home, radon, lead or other inspection. It is the home inspector's job to check on the major and minor systems in your home. No matter what condition your home is in, the home inspector will almost always find a list of issues.

Once the buyer receives the home inspection report, they will generally review it with their agent and seek advice. Often the buyer will seek to have some of the issues on the report addressed by submitting an addendum to the owner asking for those repairs to be done before the closing of the deal. It is important for you to know that you are not contractually obligated to fix anything that is found in the inspection report. At the same time, if the buyer finds issues that they cannot live with, and you do not agree to address them in any way, the buyer may terminate the transaction.

If you do receive an amendment requesting additional repairs, you will discuss your options with your agent, who will guide you in the decision-making process. Generally speaking, you can either:

1) agree to fix some or all of the items;
2) agree to provide a *cash allowance* so the buyer can address these issues after closing;
3) do a combination of 1 & 2; or
4) decide not to provide any consideration at all.

I always advise my clients to mentally set aside 1% of the sale price to address any repairs that come up during the inspection period. For example, if your home's price is $315,000, count on about $3,000 set aside (payable at closing) for inspection related issues just in case. Although I find that we seldom need that much, mentally preparing for this and considering it when accepting an offer at the start, puts you, the seller, in a better place emotionally if it does happen.

I don't recommend that you blow the deal over

inspection issues, as it is highly probable that the next buyer will have the same requests or maybe more. Minor repair issues can easily be blown out of proportion if not addressed in a way that will mentally satisfy the buyer.

On the other hand, if you have already had a pre-inspection completed on your property before putting it on the market, then you will be much further along and you will not be blindsided during this process. You will know exactly what the issues are with your home, and you can consider marketing your home as a "pre-inspected" property (kind of like a certified pre-owned luxury car).

Contract to Close

A successful and experienced Listing Agent will already have a detailed closing system in place. You would be surprised at how many deals fall apart over something so minor, but the experience and systems your agent brings to the table can all but eliminate any problems during the closing process.

The Buyer's Loan Process

If there is a purchase loan, the contract has very specific dates and requirements for the buyer to adhere to in order to satisfy the contract. While it is the buyer agent's responsibility to stay on top of these, a good listing agent never relies on that happening. They have already experienced what the public eventually finds out: namely that too many agents are part time or do almost no business in real estate, and therefore they don't have a positive impact on getting the sale to the closing table.

A good listing agent will follow up a day or two prior to each requirement needing to be completed. They will remind the buyer agent of the upcoming requirements and make sure everything is moving forward properly. For example, per our contract, the buyer must complete their physical written application for the loan within 7 calendar days of the contract being fully accepted (ratified). Your listing agent should confirm that this has happened, as well as recording the date of follow-up and the results of that follow-up.

Sadly, following up and keeping a buyer agent on task is not as easy as it might sound. If the buyer agent is part-time, the listing agent will likely have great difficulty contacting the agent or getting a return call or email. This is why the listing agent will also follow up with the buyer's lender.

After that, the agent will be following up on the buyer's appraisal being completed as well as the eventual final commitment approval for the buyer's loan. It may seem at this time that the agent is more focused on the buyer than you, the seller, and this may be true. Once there is a contract, the seller, in Virginia at least, is more or less just along for the ride. Your agent will be working with you to gather information that is needed, like your utility companies, as well as making certain, if you have an association where you live, that you order the association resale documents as required by the contract.

Mostly, you, as the seller, are packing and getting ready

for your move. However, you may at some point be working on items related to the inspection results if there are any issues. If you have a home with a well or septic tank, then it's probable that you will be paying for and ordering those inspections. If that is the case, your listing agent will work closely with you on those as well.

There are many nuances to all of this, but another important reason your listing agent should stay on top of things is in case the buyer tries to void their offer based on financing or not getting the final approval. If your listing agent is detailing what they are finding along the way, it can often take this option away from the buyer. For example, if the buyer failed to complete their written application within the 7 days required but later tried to void the offer, it is possible that you can defend against this by proving they were in default of their contractual requirement earlier.

I would love to say it is that easy, but the realities are that the contract is complex and if you yourself are not doing what is required, and when it is required, you too may be in default. A good and EXPERIENCED listing agent will be able to protect you from catastrophes and all of the potential issues that every contract brings with it.

Smoothing Out the Process

There are a few small things every seller can do as soon as they have an offer, or even before, that will make the closing move along smoothly.

- Title Insurance Policy – If it has been 10 years or less since the purchase or last refinance of your home, give a copy of your current title insurance policy to your listing agent. This will also be a nice gesture to the buyer as they can often get a discount on their portion of the title insurance if the title company managing the closing has a copy of your past policy.
- Survey – It's very important that a buyer get their own survey, but you should also find a copy of your original survey. Having this ready can help defend against inconsistencies found with the buyer's survey if any should come up that impact you in a negative way.
- Utilities – Get together a detailed list of the current utility providers for your home and their phone numbers. This will speed the process for transferring the utilities later. It's also a great idea to list any service companies you have used regularly – HVAC, Septic or Well, etc.
- Warranties – If you have appliances or systems, or perhaps a roof, that have warranties, start gathering them now. Having these during your listing phase is very helpful too.
- Association Documents – Check with your listing agent when to do this, but if you have a homeowners' or condo association, you will need to order a new copy of the association documents for the buyer.

Out of Town Sellers

Whether you are traveling at the time of your closing or have already relocated, it's important for you to know that you can close your transaction from anywhere in the United States, or internationally if you have access to a US Embassy for notary services. The escrow company can either set you up with a mobile notary or they will send the closing packet to you and you can have the documents signed at your current location in front of a U.S. notary. Many banks provide notary services at no charge.

The Day of Closing

Allow yourself about one hour to sign the closing documents. The company closing escrow will be in constant contact with you during the 48 hours prior to closing and keep you posted on the status. Sometimes the closing time or day can be delayed if the buyer's lender does not provide the closing documents to the title company in time, so be ready and know that small delays can happen.

What to bring with you to the closing:
- Valid photo ID, a driver's license or passport.
- A deposit slip for the bank to which you wish your proceeds wired.
- A blank checkbook for those last-minute emergencies that could happen during the buyer's walkthrough.
- Keys for the home. I suggest leaving all other keys, remotes, mailbox keys and manuals at the home in a drawer in the kitchen.

Fraud Alert

There is a new scam that all sellers must be aware of. Hackers are now reaching out to sellers and title companies to steal the proceeds that are due to a seller. The way they do this is by diverting the monies being wired into your bank account to be deposited to theirs. They will spoof your REALTOR®'s or title company's email (create a fake one that is really similar) and basically change the information provided to the closing attorney. Then when the closing is completed, the funds (your money) are sent to the hacker's bank account and not yours. There is no getting that money back.

To avoid this is easy. You have three options. The first is to request that the title company provide you a check to be picked up when it is ready. Then you can deposit the money directly into your account. Alternately, you can bring with you a copy of a deposit slip from your bank account and hand it directly to the title company representative when you are signing the papers at closing. The last option revolves around using caution. If you receive any communication related to your bank account details needed for wiring the funds, always call back to the title company or your REALTOR® confirming the request and supply the details to them over the phone.

12
Selling and Buying at the Same Time

Selling a home and buying a home at the same time is the most challenging situation, so it's important that you plan ahead and do everything the best way possible in order to achieve success.

All of what I am about to share is assuming that you need to sell and buy at the same time, and that you will need to use the proceeds from the sale of your current home to purchase your next home. On the other hand, if you are able to sell your current home, move in somewhere with your family, and hang out while you search for your next home, then this won't have the same impact for you, but I would still suggest that you check out some of my recommendations.

When you have to sell and buy at the same time, these are the major concerns:
- owning two homes at the same time
- having to move more than once

- losing a home that you really wanted because you couldn't sell your home in time
- becoming ensnared in a legal battle later because things fell apart and you lacked the proper protection in your contract
- trying to time these two separate real estate transactions to finish in the right order and within a very concise timeline
- and what if the buyer for your home also has a home to sell?

Should I Sell or Buy First?

Without any other considerations, you will almost always list your home for sale and find your buyer before you go looking for a home. There are two reasons this will typically be what you want to do. First, until you have an offer on your home, you are not in a strong position to purchase. Second, when you go to write an offer on a home to purchase, you will be required to disclose the fact that you have a home to sell, and most sellers are not open to this scenario. On the other hand, if you already have a buyer under contract to purchase your home, you are less of risk to the seller whose home you are trying to buy.

As you approach this challenging situation, you also need to do some quick research. All of this can be done by your selected real estate agent, and it includes the following:

Identify your market

What type of home selling market are you in? Is it a seller's market, a buyer's market or a flat market?

- In a seller's market, there is a low supply of homes and a high demand from buyers.
- In a buyer's market, there is a high number of homes for sale and a low demand for those homes.
- In a flat market, as you would assume, the supply and demand are fairly even.

Does your neighborhood and area fit into one of these market trends? You will want to make certain that your home's location is experiencing the same market that is around it. An example of when it might not fit is when you have a strong seller's market but your home is a newer home in a subdivision that is still building new homes. While the overall area is a seller's market, you may find that being so close to these new homes under construction makes your home fall into a much flatter market. This can adversely impact your time to find a buyer.

Are you moving locally, or moving out of the area?

If you are moving locally, this can make coordinating everything simpler to manage. In this situation, I would suggest that you use the same agent who will list your home for sale to also help you buy your next home. This is not the dual agency situation I tell people to avoid at all costs in the Lies and Misdirections bonus chapter of this book.

Using the same agent for both can really smooth things out for you, and having just one point of contact managing everything keeps important things from falling through the cracks. If you use two separate agents, there is a much higher risk of things going bad later, and possibly losing the buyer for your home or losing the home you are trying to purchase.

On the other hand, if you are moving out of the area, you will have two different agents helping you; and it is important that these agents are introduced to each other early on. They will need to communicate with each other to help everything run as smoothly as possible. Make sure both agents are proactive communicators and are capable of managing the interaction with the other agent effectively and to your benefit.

Are you buying a pre-existing home or a new construction?

An additional layer of challenges is added if you are purchasing a new construction. It means that the goal of moving only once is all but impossible. (Further along in this volume, I do offer some creative solutions that may help get you back to moving only once.) New construction completion dates can change without notice, and the builder's contract allows for that. Delays or early completions can quickly throw your situation into a tailspin.

I had a seller who called me only after they had written an offer to buy new construction in another state. To add to the challenges, they waited to contact me until there was only three months left before the scheduled completion date of their new home. On the surface, ninety days seems like a reasonable amount of time to sell a home in our area. But they didn't realize that their neighborhood market status was flat. They thought that it was a seller's market (though they had never confirmed that), so they had felt no urgency to reach out to me sooner. Entering the market late and pricing on the higher side of what they should have priced it was a mistake. What resulted was a seller who was having anxiety attacks due to the lack of interest in the home they were selling, and due to the fact that they could possibly lose their dream home where they were hoping to retire. Eventually, reduced pricing found a buyer, and pushing their buyer to a fast closing saved them from losing their new home. They were very fortunate to sell their house in time, but their lack of understanding and preparation caused them a great deal of stress and they lost thousands of dollars on their sale because of it.

Protecting Yourself

Your agent will help direct you regarding the contingencies you should add to any sales offer you are going to be a part of. I'll share the three common ones that are used and whether they apply to you on the selling or the buying side.

If you write an offer on a home, but you don't yet have a buyer signed for the sale of your present home, then you have what is called a Home Sale contingency. It means just that: you, the buyer, are writing the offer to buy a home, but you have a home to sell and you are still looking for a buyer for your current house. In a flat or seller's market, most sellers don't want to accept offers with this contingency. They don't want to take their home off the market while you try to find a buyer, –even in a seller's market, where you should be able to get an offer quickly. The seller and their agent don't know you, and they don't know if your home is in horrible condition, or if your price is too high, or maybe it sits under the grand central station of power lines in your county. They won't want to take the chance.

Home of Choice Contingency

If you are selling your home but have nowhere to go except to your next home after you sell, then this contingency is important. In this case, you will add language to your 'offer to sell' that says: 'I will sell my home to you but it is contingent on my ability to find a home to buy'. Then, if you, the seller, do not have an offer to purchase your next home in place in x number of days, there are two options. The first option is simply that the offer to sell becomes void and both parties can go their own ways without penalty. But most often, the second option – extending the contingency in writing by additional days – is the one that is chosen. If the buyer really wants your home, they will typically be open to an extension. Every situation is different, so working closely with your agent and keeping the lines of communication open are important.

If you are a buyer who must sell so as to use those proceeds to purchase your next home, these next two contingency options are for you. To protect yourself from legal issues, and from having to own two homes at once, the following contingencies are paramount for your protection.

Home Sale Contingency

If you don't yet have a buyer for your home, you will need this contingency in place. It discloses to the buyer that you have a home to sell and that you are still looking for a buyer; and it adds language about how many days you will have to locate a buyer. Then, if you don't have a buyer by the number of days agreed upon, the offer can be voided, or you may be able to negotiate an extension of additional days (in writing) with the seller of the home you are hoping to buy However, depending on the type of market – seller, buyer or flat – many sellers do not like this contingency. If they accept your offer and you don't locate a buyer, they may miss a window of opportunity to get the right buyer for their home. This is why having your home under contract prior to looking for a home is so important.

Coinciding Settlements Contingency

The next thing that can help you protect yourself as a buyer is the Coinciding Settlements contingency. If you already have a signed buyer for your home, this one can be used with your own offer to purchase. It discloses to the seller of the home you are buying that you have a home under contract, and that you must close on that home in order to purchase their home. This one is a bit more acceptable to sellers but it still exposes them. It states that if at any time the buyer of your home is unable to close on purchasing, you then have the right to void the offer to purchase the seller's home at no penalty. It's important to know that the language of this contingency is typically also included in the Home Sale contingency – so when you are able to remove your Home Sale contingency, you will still be protected by this clause as well.

Remember that selecting an experienced agent to help you is critical. And don't be afraid to question anything that you're not sure about. This is your sale and purchase, and if your agent misses adding something to protect you, there can be serious negative financial consequences.

Keeping Your Eye on the Big Picture

Everyone wants to win with both transactions. When selling a home, the seller wants to get the absolute highest price for their home; and when buying a home, the buyer wants to save as much money as they can. Work for a win on both, of course, but keep the reality of the markets you are in as you move forward.

On one side, you may be selling and there may be a great selling market, but then as you look to buy in the same area, you may be just one of the many buyers searching for a good home. So instead of focusing on only one of the transactions, try to see them as one large transaction where you want to win overall.

CREATIVE SOLUTIONS

Rent Back

In a seller's market, you may be in a position to request a rent back during your contract negotiations for the sale of your home. A rent back agreement is when you go to closing on the sale of your home but the buyers agree to allow you, for a fee, to stay for x number of days in the home you are selling. So, you are in fact renting back the home you just sold. If the purchase side of your sale is not able to close in time to allow you to move from one home into the next seamlessly, then a rent back agreement may be a great option for you. A buyer that really wants your home in a strong seller market may be willing to take on the aggravation of where to stay while you rent the home back – so that their offer will be selected over others.

Purchase Home Storage

This one is a bit shakier, but I've pulled it off successfully many times. There may be a situation where you will close on selling your home but then need to wait to close on your purchase. If this is the situation, you will need to find a solution for storing all of your belongings. If the property you are buying has a garage, you can ask the current owners if they would consider letting you keep some of your larger items in the garage for a short period of time. If they do agree, it's important to know that this does not automatically give you permission to return to the home at any time to get into your items that are there.

The best time to address these options is as early as possible, even during the contract negotiation phase. I have found that people are more likely to be open to these requests if they are asked sooner rather than later. People tend to become less flexible as they get farther down the road to closing.

Bonus Chapter: REALTOR® Lies and Misdirection

This was my favorite chapter to write. Having started in real estate in 2002, I have seen and heard it all. Part of what goes on in this business is the shady tactics some agents use to generate leads for their business. They offer a too-good-to-be-true scenario to get the seller to call them. Later, the seller finds out that the offer they thought would save them from being stuck with their home was a lot of smoke and mirrors.

A REALTOR® should be a professional who helps you sell or buy a home, not a snake oil salesman. Here are some of the lies and misdirections to watch out for.

Your Home on Every Website

<u>Misdirection</u>: It typically goes like this: The agent, during their presentation, tells you something miraculous. They, because they are so amazing, will get your home onto every

major website (and they imply that other agents cannot). How lucky that you found them.

Truth: The MLS backend system is integrated with a 3rd party provider that, by default, *automatically* submits your listing to all of the websites, including competing brokerage websites and the national portals. It is the *brokerage* that can edit these permissions, not that agent. While most brokerages leave the default setting, one major one is for Zillow. Our local MLS does not submit listings to Zillow by default. The funny thing is that many agents do not even know this. In order for Zillow to get the listings, their broker must login to the back end 3rd party system and approve Zillow. The problem is that even some of the smaller brokers and some larger ones are so busy with other things that they don't even know this. You *need* your home on Zillow; **it is now the #1 real estate portal online.**

Suggestion: Agents advising you your home will be on all the important websites is fine. Agents that imply they personally are the reason your home will appear on all the online real estate portals are lying to you.

We'll Buy Your Home in 90 Days

Misdirection: The agent advertises that if your home is not sold in X number of days, they will buy it from you. You have this false sense that your home is worth $500k and that they will buy it for $500k in 90 days if it doesn't sell.

Truth: This is a huge marketing ploy to get sellers to call

them. You know what they say: if it sounds too good to be true, it probably is. Here are some of the things you are likely to find out.

- Their disclaimer often states that they only offer this in a limited service area.

- It may also state that they offer this only for homes up to a certain sales point, say $250,000.

- You agree upfront to scheduled price reductions within the first 90 days.

- You agree that even at the *lowest* adjusted price, you will sell it to them at that price, not your original list price.

- You agree that despite the low price, they will still collect their full compensation fee – often 4 to 7 % of the final sales price.

- You agree that they can still find a buyer *after* they are under contract with you, and that they will keep all the profit if they sell it to that buyer at a higher price than they paid you.

Suggestion: If you every feel yourself enticed by this one, ask the agent advertising it that you want to see the full terms of that agreement before you will meet with them. I'm not sure what seller would agree to these terms ever.

I Have a Great Marketing Plan

<u>Misdirection</u>: This one I mentioned earlier. So many agents are not full time. When you meet with them, they tell you that they have great connections and a great marketing plan, but they never show you anything of value – no samples, no client testimonials.

<u>Truth</u>: You find out that their master plan for marketing is only doing what I call the 3-P's.

- They <u>**P**ut</u> your home in the MLS
- They <u>**P**lace</u> a sign in your yard
- They <u>**P**ray</u> that it sells.

This is every seller's nightmare. Their home sits on the market with no showings and no attention at all. Then after the damage has already been done, the seller eventually cancels their agreement with that agent and looks for a better solution.

<u>Suggestion</u>: Ask for samples of what they provide for their marketing. Refer to my 'Questions to Ask Every Agent' section in Chapter 6. Every agent starts somewhere but there's no reason that you should hire them while they try to learn their trade.

I Market Your Home on Social Media

<u>Misdirection</u>: During their listing appointment they mention they will add you to their Facebook, Instagram and social media pages. I'm sure you have heard that social media

advertising is important and it really is!

<u>Truth</u>: Most agents and even their brokerages don't have nearly enough followers for that to have any impact at all. What you as a seller need them to do is post an Advertisement on the social media sites that cost them money. They need to target *buyers* looking to buy a home. They should also specifically target your *neighborhood* with this ad and really boost its exposure. Most agents I speak to have NEVER placed an ad on social media, and nor could they explain how to do it.

<u>Suggestion</u>: I know you don't like sitting down and talking to all of these agents – aren't they all the same? NO, they are not! Take the time to ask for examples. Ask them to explain how things work. It should be quite clear if they are proficient or not. If they are not, often they will say something like: I've never found this to work and it's a waste of time. RED FLAG!

Dual Agency Saves You Money

<u>Misdirection</u>: Dual agency is the situation that occurs when your *listing agent* also represents the *buyer* of your home. Agents will tell you that Dual Agency is a good thing and that it saves you money and time having one agent handle it all for you. Often the Listing Agent will offer to reduce the total compensation slightly if they represent both sides.

<u>Truth</u>: Dual Agency means that neither the seller nor the

buyer receive negotiating or contract advice from the agent. Typically, what happens with Dual Agency is that the Agent is relegated to just being a paper pusher and cannot offer advice to either party. You hired your Listing Agent for advice and negotiating skills. These disappear with Dual Agency.

Suggestion: Tell your agent, right at the start when signing your listing agreement, that you are not okay with Dual Agency. What *may* be an option is having the buyer be an unrepresented party. Basically, your agent still represents only *you*, but can provide assistance to the buyer, although never in a position of offering them advice or suggestions since only *you* would be their client.

Agreeing to a High Listing Price

Misdirection: Many agents get sellers to sign listings with them, rather than the seller selecting other agents they have interviewed, by telling the seller they can sell *at a very high price.*

Truth: For some agents there is great value in just having a sign in a neighborhood or area that they are trying to generate business in. Even if the home is overpriced. The value is in the exposure to people driving by, potential buyer leads, and creating more credibility as they market to your neighbors. The problem is that the seller who was initially excited about the high price is talked into price reductions, and in the long run loses a great deal of money in the process, if they ever sell at all.

Suggestion: Never select your REALTOR® based on their suggested listing price of your home. Ask for the agent to provide details and recent sales data that supports the price they are suggesting your home will sell for. Remember, if you price too high, the damage it can do to your ability to sell and get the highest profit will take a direct hit.

I Have a Buyer for Your Home – List with Me.

Misdirection: This one is usually done via a mailer or postcard. A homeowner gets this notification from an agent stating that they have a buyer interested in buying a home in the area and that the seller should contact them if they are looking to sell.

Truth: REALTOR® Marketing 101 teaches new real estate agents to mail out to neighborhoods saying they have a buyer and if the owner is considering selling they should call the agent. Many agents even address this potential lie with their brokers. The answer they get is: well, when you list their home for sale you will in fact be marketing hard for that seller to find a buyer. No matter how you try to dress it up, it's a lie. They never actually had a specific buyer for your home.

Suggestion: Ask the agent if the buyer they have is prequalified and if you can see the prequalification letter. First you want to know: does this potentially fictitious buyer exist and does he or she have the ability to buy your home? Next, tell them to bring the buyer by to see the home. If the buyer is in fact interested in the home, you can discuss the sale at that time. But before you do, re-read the Dual Agency misdirection addressed previously.

I Save You More with My Discount Commission

Misdirection: This one will get the best and smartest of most home sellers to bite. An agent tells you that they will list your home for sale at a claimed 'discount' percent to save you even more money. Sometimes they say they are only charging 1% but fail to disclose that you will also pay an additional amount to the buyer's agent, for a total of 4-5%.

Truth: One of the main goals is to keep the seller focused on a low compensation rate and distract the seller from asking the real questions. We have all heard 'you get what you pay for' and it is so true in this situation. A seller thinks, Wow, I'm already saving 1-2%. The truth is these discount agents often lack the skill to even negotiate their own fee or prove their value to a seller when interviewing, so they lead by offering a discount in the hopes the seller won't ask too many telling questions. When problems arise in a home sale, and they often do, they then lack the experience or skill to properly protect the seller's best interest, losing the seller a lot of money along the way. Potentially they will even lose that sale. These agents are often more motivated for a fast close and want the seller to take any offer that comes along. For them, because they have heavily discounted their services, it's all about volume and getting paid, and not about the seller's best interest. Statistically, they sell for a great deal less than full-time, experienced agents – 3-6% less, causing the seller to lose 1-4% more than if they had selected an experienced full service agent.

Suggestion: Ask my questions listed in Chapter 5 of every REALTOR® you interview. Rely on their answers to select your Listing Agent. Avoid an agent who is trying to distract you from the important questions based on a discounted fee.

My Real Estate Brokerage Matters – Pick Me

Misdirection: A REALTOR® may tell you that one of the reasons they are a better choice is because they are part of the #1, biggest and best brokerage around, and that because of the X-thousands of agents they have access to, you should not consider any other agent.

Truth: First of all, when you hear this, what you should be hearing is: 'I'm not an experienced or confident agent.' Never in my career have I felt the need to use the brokerage I was with as a strength or as a reason someone should pick me. The fact is the brokerage does *nothing* to help me sell my listings. As the listing agent, I do all that work.

Second, the biggest shift for real estate started back in August 1991 when the Internet became fully accessible to the public. Twenty years after that, major real estate portals like REALTOR.com, Trulia and Zillow came along and crushed the power of the large brokerages and their local chokehold. Now every agent, even solo agents, have complete access to REALTORS® and buyers across the globe.

Third, it would be completely incorrect to imagine that an agent with ABC-Realty is better off bringing her buyers only to ABC-Realty's listings first or at all. If that were the practice, it could potentially be a conflict to their fiduciary responsibility to the buyer as well as a Fair Housing violation. Also, there cannot be any internal incentive to them as it would be unethical and illegal. Every agent looks for the best homes for their buyers regardless of the brokerage that has listed them.

The power of the Internet has created a very level playing field for the smaller brokerages to easily compete with the large branded brokerages. When you hire an agent, it is the *agent* and not the brokerage that matters. Agents are almost always independent contractors, and the good ones work hard for their clients and know their business.

One quick disclaimer about brokerages. While the brokerage should not be the reason you hire an agent, it might be a reason to look even more closely at why you might select one of their agents. The dirty secret is that as a REALTOR® I am held to a high standard and code of ethics. I'm *not* allowed to name those horrible agents and even the horrible brokerages that are out there. It is considered a violation to do that. But get a group of REALTORS® in the same soundproof room, then ask them independently to identify the worse brokerages to work with due to their agent's lack of training or ethics, and the answers will be so similar it will scare you.

Suggestion: Stick to the 11 Probing Interview Questions for REALTORS® in Chapter 5 and you will be in a great place to find the best agent, regardless of their brokerage.

Open Houses Sell Homes

Misdirection: An open house is a great tool to help you find a buyer for your home.

Truth: This is a challenging one. Open houses on average have a low success rate when it comes to generating a buyer. However, that number can change based on the location and characteristics of your neighborhood. An open house in an exclusive area in Arlington, Virginia may draw a lot of visitors and potentially offers; whereas an open house for a home in a more suburban or rural area seldom brings in qualified buyers or offers.

When an agent starts out, they are typically advised that if they want to generate buyer leads, they will have great success holding open houses. I've been around this industry for a long time, and I have yet to hear a broker or trainer tell their REALTOR® audience that one of the best tools to sell a home is an open house. They know it is not.

The success of an open house in the eyes of a homeowner and a listing agent can be completely different, and potentially even in opposition to each other's goals. The seller sees an open house as successful if they end up with an offer to purchase soon after the open house. A listing agent holding an open house sees it as successful if they can collect a few names and leads for people looking to buy a home or even sell a home.

While it is possible to find a buyer through an open house, depending on the area and the national averages, the odds are definitely against it. I have found that, the older the homeowner is, the more likely it is that they want an open house, simply because this used to be effective. Prior to the year 2000, before the Internet was such a powerful tool in the world of real estate, open houses were a necessity. Now, however, with the Internet, video, high resolution photos, and 3D home walking tours, potential buyers can easily qualify the homes they want to see in person while sitting at home or in their local coffee shop.

Suggestion: If you want an open house, be honest with yourself about where your home is located and the value of having one. Personally, I would prefer to spend that time actively marketing the home in question, rather than sitting passively inside the home hoping someone may come in and write an offer.

I Am a Million Dollar Producer

Misdirection: On their marketing material and in conversations with you they state they are a Million Dollar Agent or part of the Million Dollar Producers Club. As a non-real estate agent this sounds impression.

Truth: Most buyers and sellers think this is referring to how much the agent has earned while selling real estate. In fact all it means is that they achieved a total sales volume in one year that totaled at least one million dollars.

It's meant to be misleading because newer agents especially need some hook to make it sound like they are doing great. The truth here is that if they sell 3 homes all priced at $350,000 then they have achieved the sales volume needed to make this claim. So just about any part time agent out there that sells 3-4 homes in a year can say they are part of the Million Dollar Producers Club.

<u>Suggestion:</u> Ignore all of the distractions agents might throw your way and stick to the 11 Probing Interview Questions to help you locate a strong, experienced agent to help you sell your home quickly.

Conclusion...

All my time working as a Listing Agent has shown me one thing: Sellers do a really bad job of selecting their Listing Agent. But it's not your fault. When it is time to sell, there are so many other things on your mind. REALTOR's® media and mass marketing make it hard to stop and think of the real reason you are hiring them. But now you have more information so you can be part of the new wave of informed sellers. Armed with this knowledge, you can easily filter through agents you meet with and quickly find the best one for you.

Since selling your home is a life event, and will likely be your single largest transaction representing your biggest asset, your commitment to educating yourself on the process is wise, and I commend you for trying to do it right. Doing this *does* take effort, but doing this right will allow you to sell your home the first time and will absolutely put the most money back into your pocket.

I wish you the best of luck, and if you have any real estate related questions please contact me.

Limits of Liability & Disclaimer of Warranty

Now you are seeing the tough part of Real Estate and being a REALTOR®. We always need to remind people that we are not attorneys, tax consultants, rocket scientists and more. When entering a real estate transaction, I highly recommend that you consult a local broker or real estate attorney. The contents of this book are offered as informational and educational material only.

Copyright

Copyright © 2017 Steve Bradley

For information about permission to reproduce selections from this book, write to Realtor@gotoBGR.com

How to Contact the Author

STEVE BRADLEY

Principal Real Estate Broker

Bradley Group Realtors

Manassas, Virginia USA

Email: Realtor@gotoBGR.com

Phone: (571) 379-5424 – office

Web: www.gotoBGR.com

Facebook: www.facebook.com/BradleyGroupRealtors

Facebook: www.facebook.com/HomeSellingSurvivalGuide

LinkedIn: www.linkedin.com/in/RealtyExpert1

YouTube: www.youtube.com/user/BradleyGroupRealtors

Made in the USA
Middletown, DE
28 March 2019